ICE AGE MEGA BEASTS

DIRE WOLVES

by Sara Gilbert

CREATIVE EDUCATION • CREATIVE PAPERBACKS

Published by Creative Education and Creative Paperbacks
P.O. Box 227, Mankato, Minnesota 56002
Creative Education and Creative Paperbacks are
imprints of **The Creative Company**
www.thecreativecompany.us

Design and production by **Chelsey Luther**
Art direction by **Rita Marshall**
Printed in the **United States of America**

Photographs by Alamy (Chronicle, Heritage Image Partnership Ltd, The
Natural History Museum, North Wind Picture Archives, Stocktrek Images, Inc.),
Corbis (Ted Soqui), Dreamstime (Artesiawells, Tranac, Yuliaavgust, Zzizar),
FreeVectorMaps.com, Getty Images (Dorling Kindersley, Mark
Hallett Paleoart)

Library of Congress Cataloging-in-Publication Data
Gilbert, Sara.
Dire wolves / Sara Gilbert.
p. cm. — (Ice age mega beasts)
Includes bibliographical references and index.
Summary: An elementary exploration of dire wolves, focusing on fossil
evidence that helps explain how their shaggy hair, strong jaws, and sharp
teeth helped these beasts adapt to the last Ice Age.

ISBN 978-1-60818-765-2 (hardcover)
ISBN 978-1-62832-373-3 (pbk)
ISBN 978-1-56660-807-7 (eBook)
1. Dire wolf—Juvenile literature. 2. Animals, Fossil—Juvenile literature. 3.
Wolves. 4. Prehistoric animals.

QE882.C15 G55 2017
569.77—dc23   2016014627

CCSS: RI.1.1, 2, 3, 4, 5, 6, 7, 10; RI.2.1, 2, 4, 5, 6, 7, 10; RI.3.1, 2, 4, 5, 7, 10;
RF.1.1, 2, 3, 4; RF.2.3, 4; RF.3.3, 4

First Edition HC 9 8 7 6 5 4 3 2 1
First Edition PBK 9 8 7 6 5 4 3 2 1

Contents

Hungry Pack

It's cold on the North American plains. But the furry bison don't mind. Neither does the *pack* of dire wolves. They are hungry. The bison will be a delicious dinner.

Strong dire wolves weighed about 175 pounds (79.4 kg).

The name "dire wolf" means "fearsome dog." Dire wolves had long bodies, shaggy hair, and sharp teeth. They looked like big, mean dogs.

Dire wolves were slightly bigger than their living gray wolf relatives.

Dogs of the Ice Age

Dire wolves lived more than 100,000 years ago. Huge sheets of ice called glaciers covered much of the northern lands then. It was a time called the Ice Age.

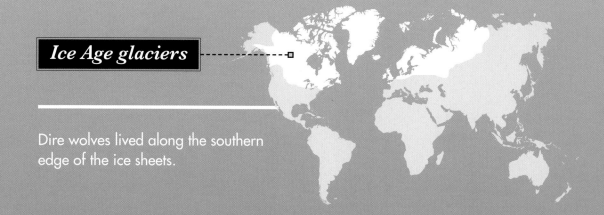

Ice Age glaciers

Dire wolves lived along the southern edge of the ice sheets.

Predators such as dire wolves and saber-toothed cats liked the cold. They hunted woolly mammoths, mountain goats, and muskoxen. The wolves fought with lions and bears.

Meat-eating predators are also known as carnivores.

From Mountains to Plains

Dire wolves could live anywhere they found *prey*. They lived in mountains and on flat plains. *Fossils* of their bones have been found from Canada to South America.

Canada

Most dire wolves lived in present-day North America.

South America

The first dire wolf fossil was found in 1854. Hundreds of fossils come from California. The wolves got stuck in pits of tar long ago.

More than 4,000 dire wolf fossils have been found in California's La Brea Tar Pits.

Bone Crushers

Dire wolves were long and strong. They had sharp teeth for slicing meat. Their teeth and strong jaws were good for crushing bone.

Like today's wolves, dire wolves hunted in packs to bring down large prey.

The wolves were strong enough to hunt huge animals. But they had to eat fast. Other predators fought them for the same food!

Saber-toothed cats and teratorns competed with dire wolves for food.

When the Ice Age ended, the Earth warmed. The largest animals disappeared. About 10,000 years ago, the dire wolf died out, too.

Gray wolves came on the scene before the last dire wolves died out.

Dire Wolf Close-up

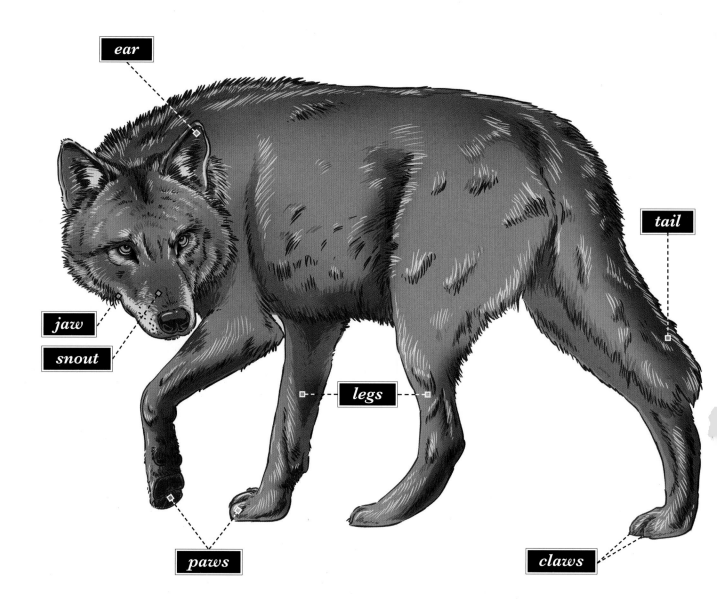

ear

jaw

snout

tail

legs

paws

claws

Glossary

fossils: remains of animals or plants

pack: a group of wild animals that hunts together

predators: animals that hunt other animals for food

prey: animals that are hunted and eaten by other animals

Read More

Lindsay, William. *Eyewitness Prehistoric Life.* New York: DK, 2012.

Turner, Alan. *National Geographic Prehistoric Mammals.* Washington, D.C.: National Geographic, 2004.

Websites

Enchanted Learning: Ice Age Mammals
http://www.enchantedlearning.com/subjects /mammals/Iceagemammals.shtml
Learn more about the Ice Age and the animals that lived then.

Illinois State Museum: Wolves, Coyotes, and Dogs
http://exhibits.museum.state.il.us/exhibits /larson/canis.html
See dire wolf fossils and drawings of the animal.

Index